TAKE GOD

AT HIS WORD

BOOK 2: EXPECT A HARVEST

DR. KREGG HOOD

SWEET
PUBLISHING

TAKE GOD AT HIS WORD, BOOK 2:
Expect a Harvest

Copyright © 2001 by Sweet Publishing
5750 Stratum Drive
Fort Worth, TX 76137
1-800-531-5220

ISBN: 0-8344-0273-4

Printed in the U. S. A.

03   04   05   06   ❖   6   5   4   3

CONTENTS

HOW TO GET THE MOST FROM TAKE GOD AT HIS WORD 2

Follow these guidelines faithfully, and you'll take a major step forward in your walk with the Lord.

1. Read one chapter each week. Take time on Monday or Tuesday to read. This will allow more process time. If you have a family, take turns reading the chapter out loud together.

2. Discuss the principles with close friends or family members. If you have children living at home, include them, too. It's especially valuable to meet "around the kitchen table" at least one evening each week. The questions at the end of each chapter are designed to help you see God as the source of your blessings. Talk and pray together about your experiences with money and giving. Discuss your parents' influence, too. If married, note the areas in which you and your mate agree, as well as where you disagree. Continue to talk and pray about the points you disagree on until God leads you to a place of unity.

3. Pray for God's wisdom regarding financial matters. Invest time praying about your needs, spending, giving, and overall financial attitudes and habits. Ask God to guard your heart from fears that keep you from trusting him with your giving decisions. Give him these fears and ask him for wisdom and strength.

May the Lord bless you as you set out on a
new journey of faith!

GOD PROMISES TO PROVIDE

You may think that this book is about giving, but it's more about receiving. God wants us to receive all the physical, emotional, and spiritual benefits and blessings he has to give. They are freely given. But we do have a price to pay—we have to believe God will make good on his promises. We have to trust God enough to take him at his word. If he says he will do it, we can take it to the bank, both literally and figuratively.

Jesus said, "Give, and it will be given to you. A good measure, pressed down, shaken together and running over, will be poured into your lap. For with the measure you use, it will be measured to you."

This promise from Luke 6:38 has the power to change lives! God makes this promise because he wants to give Christians greater provision, and he wants to break the bondage that fear has placed over our financial lives. Knowing that we need motivation and encouragement, he promises that if we will turn loose of our hard earned money, especially in scarce times, and abandon our self-reliance, he will make it worth our while. Read again the phrase about what will come back to you: "Pressed down, shaken together and running over." This is an image of overflowing abundance. God is not stingy. He will flood us with blessings when we trust his word in giving.

Give, and it will be given to you. A good measure, pressed down, shaken together and running over, will be poured into your lap. For with the measure you use, it will be measured to you.

Luke 6:38

Let's Pray

Lord, your Word says, "Give and it will be given to you." That is an amazing and challenging promise! I know you are the Source of every good gift. And I believe it is your heart to take care of me and my loved ones. I know this because you are a faithful, promise-keeping God. Thank you, Lord, in advance, for the new and exciting truths you will share with me in the next few minutes of reading. God, I actually want you to stretch my faith and deepen my commitment to you. I know that request can be a bit scary, but with you in charge, I'm confident of the results. In Jesus' name. Amen.

CHAPTER ONE:
Give and It Will Be Given to You

God is amazing! I love to find out about times when he shows us just how many ways he can meet our needs and let us experience the power of giving. Stan Tolar tells of the time when he and his wife felt the Lord wanted them to give $50 to some missionary friends of theirs. Their own checkbook only had $54 in it but they decided to trust God and mail the check, even though they wondered exactly how they would manage. The very next day Stan went to the mailbox and found a letter in the mailbox from one of his old college roommates. The letter read, "Stan, I just had you and Linda on my heart and felt impressed to write you. I'm enclosing a check for you, knowing you will probably put it in the offering plate next Sunday, but it is not for your church. It is for you." The letter contained a check for—you guessed it—fifty bucks!

But the story was far from over. When the check the Tolars sent to their missionary friends arrived, their friend called immediately and said, "Stan, your check just arrived. What timing! We had a doctor's appointment for our daughter, Angie, but we had no money to pay the bill. I was just about to make the dreaded phone call to cancel, but I paused to look at the mail first and there it was. The Lord was right on schedule, wasn't he?"[1]

Isn't God amazing? Not only did he meet the physical needs of two families, he blessed a third person in the process. Only God is this powerful and creative.

I know of many other stories like this one that illustrate God's faithful provision. They are all examples of the word God wants us to believe: "Give and it will be given to you."

Even though this book is about giving our resources to accomplish Kingdom purposes, this form of giving is actually a pathway to greater blessing than we could have ever dreamed possible.

God has given you several promises that you can grab hold of during lean times in your finances. These words from him will sustain you and focus your attention on how you act in faith, even when you experience fear and doubt.

Very simply, God gives his word:

1. "Give and it will be given to you" (Luke 6:38). You really can't outgive God. The more you give, the more he will sustain, enrich, and empower your life.

2. "Let me prove it to you" (Malachi 3:10). If you'll begin to give at least a tenth of your income, God will prove his fantastic ability to bless.

3. "Take hold of true life" (1 Timothy 6:19). Once we begin to overcome the hold that financial issues have over us, we move into levels of greater blessings such as

contentment and generosity, helping us enjoy what God gives us.

4. "Expect a harvest" (Matthew 13:23). God's law of the universe, you reap what you sow (Galatians 6:7), is unchanged through time and no act of obedient faith goes unnoticed by him. When you sow seed for God, begin to look for a harvest. It's on the way!

Take a Step into God's Power

God wants to trust you and me with his resources. That's one of the reasons why Luke 6:38 has come to mean so much to me. Jesus said, "Give, and it will be given to you. A good measure, pressed down, shaken together and running over, will be poured into your lap. For with the measure you use, it will be measured to you."

This phrase reminds me of what I see when I open a new box of breakfast cereal. It looks half-full! Of course I know what has happened. The machines used to blow dry cereal into the boxes don't pack the cereal in. So, by the time a box reaches the grocery story shelves, the contents have settled. So a "full" box looks half-empty.

God is not like that. He pours out blessing and packs it down. Then he pours out more blessing until it overflows our capacity to hang on to it. Let me illustrate. When I went off to college for my senior year, I packed all my clothes, pictures, a refrigerator, books, bookcases, and a stereo system, including two very large speakers into my two door, 1972 Monte Carlo. I used every space you could imagine to transport my belongings to campus. When I arrived and started to unload, it seemed I would never finish making trips back and forth from the car. My "stuff" was pressed down, shaken together, and running over. I still don't know how I got all those things in that car! Do you see this picture? This is the way God works. He wants to heap blessing upon blessing on us.

Many other passages in the Bible reflect this level of abundant care:

> Honor the LORD with your wealth,
>   with the firstfruits of all your crops;
> then your barns will be filled to
>   overflowing,
> and your vats will brim over with
>   new wine.
>
> (Proverbs 3:9-10)

You may say to yourself, "My power and the strength of my hands have produced this wealth for me." But remember the LORD your God, for it is he who gives you the ability to produce wealth, and so confirms his covenant, which he swore to your forefathers, as it is today.

> (Deuteronomy 8:17-18)

> Wealth and honor come from you;
>   you are the ruler of all things.
> In your hands are strength and power
>   to exalt and give strength to all.
>
> (1 Chronicles 29:12)

But seek first his kingdom and his righteousness, and all these things will be given to you as well.

> (Matthew 6:33)

Now he who supplies seed to the sower and bread for food will also supply and increase your store of seed and will enlarge the harvest of your righteousness. You will be made rich in every way so that you can be generous on every occasion, and through us your generosity will result in thanksgiving to God.

(2 Corinthians 9:10-11)

And my God will meet all your needs according to his glorious riches in Christ Jesus.

(Philippians 4:19)

Some think these passages have no bearing on physical blessing but that God is referring to spiritual or emotional benefits.

I agree that Jesus' statement in Luke 6 represents a general principle about God's responding to our faithfulness in giving. And, since it is a general principle, it would include *all ways* God blesses, including financial. People can make two mistakes while attempting to understand the application of this verse: thinking it refers *only* to money (both giving and receiving) and thinking it excludes money. As is true in so many principles, the truth is found balanced between the two extremes. God has concern for your physical needs and will meet those needs.

In Luke 6:38 Jesus is also referring to receiving blessing that is measurable. He said, "With the same *measure* you use, it will be measured to you." Physical or material blessings are tangible and more easily measured than more subjective or intangible blessings. Subjective blessings can be more easily specified than quantified.

The physical results God provides are much easier to recognize. Once we begin to see the results of giving in a physical area, such as our wallet, we will gain faith and greater discernment to better see and appreciate the more subjective spiritual and emotional blessings God sends in response.

And, I've also noticed that the people concerned about this verse's being applied to physical wealth often express a doubt like, "Well, I've never seen this happen." They are saying that they allow their experience to govern their theology, rather than allowing their theology to prepare them for a new faith experience. This is the nature of faith. Hebrews 11:1 says "faith is being sure of what we hope for and certain of what we do not see." The next verse says, "This is what the ancients were commended for." So, if the saints of God long ago pleased God for believing what he told them, even though it had not yet occurred or been a part of their experience, don't you think God would be pleased with us today if we believed what he said, in spite of what our current experiences have been up to this point?

Perhaps we must be willing to believe things that have not yet happened to keep our prayer requests from being worthless. Maybe that's one of the reasons why so many of us struggle with our prayer lives. How can we believe in, ask for, and anticipate God's extraordinary or, supernatural response if we restrict him to only the natural solutions that fit within our narrow scope of knowledge and experience?

Which sentence sounds more like God's approach?
1—You must see in order to believe, or
2—You must believe in order to see.

The Bible tells of numerous individuals who practiced the first one—the Israelites when Moses first came to them (Exodus 4:5), the queen of Sheba (1 Kings 10:7), Zechariah, the father of John the Baptist (Luke 1:20, 63-64), the disciples on the road to Emmaus (Luke 24:25), Nicodemus (John 3:12), Mary and Martha (John 11:40), Thomas (John 20:27, 29), and others.

God had great compassion for each of these saints in their struggle with doubt and fear. He guided them through their unbelief, just as he will guide us through ours. But we must be willing to trust and *take a step forward* in order to experience God's greater blessing.

If you choose the second statement as your personal goal, it can be well supported in Scripture by:

- The blind men who wanted to see (Matthew 9:28)

- The way Jesus told us to pray (Matthew 21:22)

- The father of the boy with a fierce demon (Mark 9:24)

- Jairus, whose daughter had died (Luke 8:50)

- Paul (Ephesians 1:18-19)

- The church in Thessalonica (1 Thessalonians 2:13) and many more who believed by faith, not sight or experience.

Doesn't it also makes sense to view statement 2 as the gateway to more blessings from God? Take God at his word and believe that he will provide for you when you give.

Traps You Can Avoid

Without the practice of increased giving, Satan has a foothold into your heart and life. When you don't give, you'll not only miss out on many of the blessings God wants you to have, enjoy, and use for his glory, but you'll put yourself at risk of falling into three dangerous traps.

Trap 1—An Independent Spirit

The whole point of this book is to help us see the need to rely on God for everything. As I mentioned in the first book, God is the Source of all our blessings. He uses a variety of means to get these blessings into our lives: circumstances, opportunities, connections, jobs, bank accounts, possessions, our intelligence, training, skills, and other physical resources are his "delivery system," much like some companies who use a fulfillment warehouse to get their goods to customers. If the customers need to make another order later, they don't contact the warehouse; they go back to the source, the company. It's the same with us. We don't put our confidence in the delivery system or warehouse; we put our confidence in the God who provides these resources. I'm still drawn to Deuteronomy 8:17-18. It says, "You may say to yourself, 'My power and the strength of my hands have produced this wealth for me.' But remember the LORD your God, for it is he who gives you the ability to produce wealth, and so confirms his covenant, which he swore to your forefathers, as it is today."

In fact, in almost every church where I preach about giving, I emphasize this passage. Our American culture is so enamored with the job market and the economic indices that economists refer to the "creation of wealth."

Politicians get reelected by taking credit for the number of jobs they help to create. As individuals we can fall prey to the thought that we did it ourselves. It reminds me of the classic movie, *Shenandoah*. The leading character, played by Jimmy Stewart, opens the film with a prayer of thanksgiving for a meal. He calls the family in, makes the kids sit still, and prays, "Lord, we plowed the field, we planted the field, we harvested the crop. We cooked it and put it on the table. It wouldn't be here if it weren't for our hard work. But we thank you for it anyway. Amen." We chuckle at the scene, but I suspect Jimmy Stewart's character is illustrating the attitude on many Christians' hearts: God's material blessings are only indirect at best.

Eradicate this mind-set from your conscious or subconscious mind by making a commitment to give every Sunday (1 Corinthians 16:1-2). And as you make your offering, thank God for your job or other sources of income, reflect on the goodness of his provision for you, and trust him to replenish your resources. We must transform our thinking in order to draw our security from God. Thinking that our security is in our jobs, our friends, our abilities, or anyone else is not only a trap— it's a lie from the devil. There is no security except in the Lord.

Trap 2—Materialism

We live in a high-pressure, consumer-oriented society. Without making generous giving an essential part of our lives, we are tempted to overspend and undersave. Advertising constantly bombards us with persuasive messages manipulating our selfish desires, causing us to desire more than we need and more than what is good for us. Consumer credit card debt is at an all time high. Personal bankruptcy rates are soaring. Families are strained as expenses shrink their capability to save for the future, prepare for emergencies, or even make it to the next week.

A church member told me one Sunday that he was going to the horse races to bet on the ponies. He said he really needed to win the stake so he could pay his bills! It's hard to imagine a more foolish or dangerous plan for dealing with financial trouble.

Greed causes materialism. Greed is more than an unhealthy desire for more stuff. It's a false god that attracts our worship. In the midst of strong instruction against sinful behavior, Paul talked about greed. He wrote, "Put to death, therefore, whatever belongs to your earthly nature: sexual immorality, impurity, lust, evil desires and greed, which is idolatry. Because of these, the wrath of God is coming" (Colossians 3:5-6).

How much more encouragement do you need? One of the best ways to demolish this idol is to worship God with our heartfelt songs, fervent prayers, and wholehearted giving. When you see giving as an act of worship, it will change your heart. Philippians 4:18 says, "They [financial gifts] are a fragrant offering, an acceptable sacrifice, pleasing to God."

Whenever you struggle with greed, increase your giving! Giving is the spiritual weapon you need to tear this stronghold from your life (2 Corinthians 10:3-5). God will help you, too. If materialism has robbed you of your joy in Christ, take back your birthright as a child of the King.

Trap 3—Inadequate Provision

Are you in a financial bind? Take inventory of your giving practices. Tough times financially can come as a test from the Lord to strengthen us for greater purposes, yet most financial difficulties are directly related to our lack of giving to God.

Jesus said "With the measure you use, it will be measured to you" (Luke 6:38). His comment can be taken two ways: Increase the measure, or give more to God so he can give more back. I like the old story of the believer who was asked how he could keep giving so much of his wealth to the Lord's work. He replied, "As I shovel it out, he shovels it in, and the Lord has a bigger shovel."

This is what Paul wanted to get across to the Corinthian church. Notice how similar this passage is to Luke 6:38. "Remember this: Whoever sows sparingly will also reap sparingly, and whoever sows generously will also reap generously" (2 Corinthians 9:6).

In essence, Paul says that puny harvests are the result of meager sowing. Since the context of this passage is clearly about giving resources, it's safe to conclude that he was referring to physical resources as the harvest he would receive. Poor giving leads to poor receiving. Generous giving leads to generous receiving. When you give, God responds. He loves you and wants to care for you.

God Wants to Give You Greater Faith

"Give and it will be given to you" starts with greater provision in your personal physical life. And this is only the "ground floor" of God's blessing. It's even more important to God that he increase your faith. Notice the verb tense. That means it hasn't happened yet. You give first and then you wait until the harvest comes. Jesus used the future tense three times in this verse: It will be given, it will be poured, and it will be measured.

Only a young child would expect to plant a seed and get an immediate harvest. It takes time. With the Lord, the time between when you sow and when you reap is called faith. It's what you hope for (Hebrews 11:1). The greater the time, the greater the faith.

All committed Christians want greater faith. The problem with this desire is that it is not fulfilled easily or automatically. You can't study your way to more faith like you can study Bible facts. Faith isn't learned academically; it's developed experientially.

My ministry focus in giving has shifted dramatically over the years. When I first started preaching, I thought people didn't give because they weren't committed to God. So I preached on commitment, duty, and obligation until I started wondering why this approach didn't work. It was only then that I realized most Christians don't give because of faith. They are afraid God won't meet their needs if they give—especially if they tithe. They're afraid they won't be able to make the house payment or pay the doctor or save for college tuition. Their fear fights with their faith, keeping faith little and weak even though God is big and strong. God wants to change this small view of himself.

Jesus helped his disciples to greater faith by telling them: "So watch yourselves. If your brother sins, rebuke him, and if he repents, forgive him. If he sins against you seven times in a day, and seven times comes back to you and says, 'I repent,' forgive him" (Luke 17:3-4). What he was asking them to do was impossible from a human perspective. How does someone keep forgiving a person so often? The disciples must have felt the double bind. On the one hand, Jesus, their Lord, is commanding them to forgive someone who may be driving them crazy. They know they can't refuse Jesus' instruction. On the other hand, they know they don't have it in them to be this forgiving. The person under question could be impossible to forgive, they may have reasoned. Realizing that they didn't have the capacity within themselves to obey the Lord, they did the right thing. They asked him for greater faith to take this hard step of continual forgiveness and to believe it would do any good.

If Jesus were like today's typical preacher, he would have titled this message, "How to Forgive the Unforgivable," and then given them three steps to forgiving others, including several great illustrations to prove it can be done. Or, like many counselors today, he might have had the disciples join his forgiveness support group. Or he could have just told them do it or else!

My comments are tongue-in-cheek, of course. I like good sermons, appreciate the ministry of support groups, and understand that sometimes we have to get over our pride and do the hard thing. But, upon further review, I really like the way Jesus handled their request for greater faith. He didn't tell them an answer. He showed them. He replied, "If you have faith as small as a mustard seed, you can say to this mulberry tree, 'Be uprooted and planted in the sea, and it will obey you'" (Luke 17:6). In essence, Jesus encouraged growing and stretching our faith in the areas of our concern. With mustard-seed-sized faith, you can grab hold of a giant-sized need and go for it. Whatever the need, exercise your faith in that area.

When I think of concerns where I need greater faith, I

think about more than my financial needs. I think about the faith needed for other matters that are even greater. For example, many Christians struggle to truly believe they are saved and forgiven. What do they need? Greater faith! Or what about prayer? What do we need when praying for wisdom in a difficult circumstance or for a loved one who is sick? More faith! How about the need for evangelism and revival in our land? What does it take to fulfill 2 Chronicles 7:14: "If my people, who are called by my name, will humble themselves and pray and seek my face and turn from their wicked ways, then will I hear from heaven and will forgive their sin and will heal their land." Once again, when we learn to trust God and have faith for finances, we will have greater faith for other matters, too.

God Wants to Give You a Greater Impact on Others

The strong appeal of Luke 6:38 is that we can see the benefits to ourselves, our families, and the people who are the recipients of the resources we give. Obviously, God does not need anything we might give him. He owns everything and can make anything! As Stephen said to the Jewish leaders of the Sanhedrin, "However, the Most High does not live in houses made by men. As the prophet says: 'Heaven is my throne, and the earth is my footstool. What kind of house will you build for me? says the Lord. Or where will my resting place be? Has not my hand made all these things?'" (Acts 7:48-50). So, giving supplies nothing for God.

Luke 6:38 shows us the true importance of giving. Sure, giving allows us to receive, and giving causes our faith to grow. But most of all, giving allows us to synchronize our hearts with God's heart. The greatest giving passage is actually John 3:16: "For God so loved the world that he gave his one and only Son, that whoever believes in him shall not perish but have eternal life." Even this passage in Luke 6 is preceded by a teaching on forgiving. Immediately before Jesus tells his followers to give physical resources, he tells them to give forgiveness. "Do not judge, and you will not be judged. Do not condemn, and you will not be condemned. Forgive, and you will be forgiven" (Luke 6:37). God is sending us a message loud and clear. Give so that others can be blessed.

God wants us to become more like him and he is, by nature, a giver. He gives even beyond the point of sacrifice. "He who did not spare his own Son, but gave him up for us all—how will he not also, along with him, graciously give us all things?" (Romans 8:32). God's heart is greatly pleased when we choose to become channels of blessing instead of mere reservoirs. The difference is striking. A channel carries the water; a reservoir stores it. Think of yourself as a pipe through which his blessings flow. Don't focus on how much or how little God may want to flow through your life. Volume will vary from time to time as long as you live. Instead, pay attention to what you want your capacity to be.

I've heard John Maxwell put it this way, "Don't give to get. Give to get to give again." God wants our giving to be like breathing—inhaling and exhaling. We would suffocate without the steady exchange of air, taking in and giving out.

God sees our financial decisions the same way. If we take in and spend on ourselves and don't put a portion of the resources he has given us back into use for others, he'll slow down on what he provides. However, if we'll make and keep our financial commitments and stretch our faith toward God's purposes, he will partner with us.

The more we work together with God, the more he will do through us. Let God give this blessing to you.

Notes:
[1] Stan Tolar, as seen in "The Peter Principle," *Leadership Journal* (Fall 1998), 69.

Think It Through
Give and It Will Be Given to You

1. As you reflect on the three areas where God wants to give to you, how are you doing?

   - How has he provided for your physical needs?
   - How has he given you greater faith?
   - How has he offered you opportunities to serve others for him?

2. What lies does Satan tell people to keep them from giving? Which one of these is the biggest temptation for you?

3. In what specific area do you need help from God right now? Ask him for a breakthrough today.

4. How do you think the Lord wants you to put this chapter's teaching into practice?

"Bring the whole tithe into the storehouse, that there may be food in my house. Test me in this," says the LORD Almighty, "and see if I will not throw open the floodgates of heaven and pour out so much blessing that you will not have room enough for it."

Malachi 3:10

Let's Pray

God, you never cease to amaze me! I'm about to read and study a passage from your Scripture that says you want me to test you with my giving. It is humbling to think that you are actually saying to me, "Let me prove it to you." That's why I want to follow you more fully in my giving—to be the faithful recipient of even more of your blessings. Father, I do seek your physical provision and protection, but I have an even stronger desire to receive the more important blessings you have for me. Bless my study now and help me obey you completely. In the name of my Savior and Friend, Jesus. Amen.

CHAPTER TWO:
Let Me Prove It to You

When I was a kid I remember vividly how we boys used to talk big about what we could do on the baseball diamond. Of course, once one of us popped off about our ball-playing prowess, another boy in the group was bound to say, "Prove it!" Then the fun began. It was time to put up or shut up. More often than not, the big talk was just that—big talk. We couldn't back up our words with action.

That's one of the amazing things about God. He never fails to back up his words—with action. One of the most exciting promises he makes is found in Malachi 3 where he talks about what will happen when his people give a "tithe" or 10 percent of their income back to him. Verse 10 says,

> "Bring the whole tithe into the storehouse, that there may be food in my house. Test me in this," says the LORD Almighty, "and see if I will not throw open the floodgates of heaven and pour out so much

blessing that you will not have room enough for it."

The New International Version translates this interesting little phrase "test me in this" but the original language of the Old Testament can just as easily and accurately be translated, "Let me prove it to you." Isn't that surprising? God was inviting his people to put him to the test about tithing. In this particular context, he wanted them to trust him and take at least 10 percent of their crops into the temple storehouse. Once they did this, God told them two things would happen: ministry could be done (food in the storehouse) and they would be blessed beyond measure ("you will not have enough room for it").

Usually, it is God who tests us, as David mentioned in Psalm 139:23, "Search me, O God, and know my heart; test me and know my anxious thoughts." The word *test* carries the idea of examination and checking something out to see if it's genuine. So when God used the same word for *test* in the Malachi passage, he was giving his people an opportunity to check him out and see, firsthand, if he would be faithful.

So the question is, what exactly does God want to prove? Studying the themes of Malachi may lead you to think that the emphasis goes the other direction: Israel needed to prove some things to God or else he would have every right to destroy them. Almost the entire book of Malachi is a description of the lack of faithfulness of God's people. They were moral and spiritual failures. The people offered blind, crippled, and diseased animals to God for sacrifice. They treated marriage lightly, making divorce a frequent occurrence. Their religious teachers were indifferent to God and the people blindly followed their leaders!

In this setting God expresses his displeasure over their lack of faithfulness in giving a tithe of their crops and income back to him. Yet in spite of blatant violations of their covenant relationship with God, the Lord continued to reach out to Israel in love and mercy. Their disobedience in giving becomes their invitation to return to God. When they return to him in giving their tithes and offerings, he proves, once again, just how much he loves them.

God Longs to Bless His People

The first thing God wants to prove is that he is a God who blesses his children immensely. This promise of "so much blessing" sent me scurrying to my concordance to learn more about how God provides good things for his people. I found an enormously diverse treasure chest full of God's blessings—physical, emotional, and spiritual. Over 300 verses describe the vast extent of God's blessings.

Physical Blessings God Provides

God grants both physical and material blessings to his children. Here are a few:

Increased wealth (Deuteronomy 8:12-18; 2 Chronicles 31:10; Psalm 132:15; Proverbs 10:22)

Increased crops (Genesis 26:12; Deuteronomy 16:15; Psalm 65:10)

Increased herds (Genesis 24:35; Job 1:10;

Psalm 107:38)

Increased population (Genesis 26:24; Deuteronomy 7:13; Joshua 17:14)

The ability to bear children (Deuteronomy 28:4)

Physical health (Exodus 23:25)

Household matters (Genesis 39:5)

Food and water (Exodus 23:25)

Physical labor (Deuteronomy 2:7; Job 1:10)

Physical skills (Deuteronomy 33:11; Psalm 128:2)

Rain (Deuteronomy 33:13; Psalm 65:10; Hebrews 6:7)

Protection (1 Chronicles 4:10)

One of the most exciting passages I found was in Deuteronomy 28:2-6, 8, 12-14. Drink in the goodness of God with this reading:

All these blessings will come upon you and accompany you if you obey the LORD your God: You will be blessed in the city and blessed in the country. The fruit of your womb will be blessed, and the crops of your land and the young of your livestock—the calves of your herds and the lambs of your flocks. Your basket and your kneading trough will be blessed. You will be blessed when you come in and blessed when you go out. The LORD will send a blessing on your barns and on everything you put your hand to. The LORD your God will bless you in the land he is giving you. The LORD will open the heavens, the storehouse of his bounty, to send rain on your land in season and to bless all the work of your hands. You will lend to many nations but will borrow from none. The LORD will make you the head, not the tail. If you pay attention to the commands of the LORD your God that I give you this day and carefully follow them, you will always be at the top, never at the bottom. Do not turn aside from any of the commands I give you today, to the right or to the left, following other gods and serving them.

Doesn't that make you feel good about the benefits of obeying God? It makes me want to do whatever it takes to stand under the shower of his blessings.

Emotional Blessings

In addition to the physical blessings God promises, I notice how God enhances our quality of life by blessing our minds and emotions. For example, David wrote in Psalm 1:1-3,

> Blessed is the man
> who does not walk in the counsel
> of the wicked
> or stand in the way of sinners
> or sit in the seat of mockers.
> But his delight is in the law of the
> LORD,
> and on his law he meditates day
> and night.
> He is like a tree planted by streams

of water,
which yields its fruit in season
and whose leaf does not wither.
Whatever he does prospers.

Do you realize the happy by-products of following God's direction? When God's instructions are ignored, the door to the counsel of the wicked is opened. The counsel of the wicked directs peoples toward rage, greed, dishonesty, marital infidelity, hatred, and more. Satan works overtime manipulating us with fear, guilt, inferiority, and resentment toward others. Out of this "counsel" is every kind of pain, hurt, and disappointment known to man. We not only fail God, we cooperate with the devil.

But turn this coin over and see the benefits that come to one whose delight is in the Lord and his ways. He or she is calmer, more peaceful, a better friend, employee, family member, and neighbor. Because this person meditates on the words of God, wisdom and insight come more frequently for personal decisions. And, because of the emotionally stable foundation God gives, hard times won't cause this person to wilt under pressure. On the contrary, Scripture says, "Whatever he does prospers."

I've been given many opportunities to talk to non-Christians about why I'm a Christian. Besides expressing my gratitude for knowing that I'm going to heaven, I also tell how the Lord helps me as a husband, father, friend, leader, and worker. Even though I've made plenty of mistakes, I know that following God has protected me from many more heartaches, sins, pitfalls, and foolish activities. Knowing that my life is blessed in more ways than I can count is actually worth far more to me than anything money can buy.

Scripture is packed with examples and descriptions of blessings God gives to our inner being. Psalm 3:8 promises us access to God's deliverance. This includes power over sin and other attacks from the devil. Psalm 5:12 says God surrounds us with his favor as a shield. This exciting verse tells us to expect God to cause good things to happen in our personal relationships, our jobs, and other daily circumstances. Psalm 29:11 says God gives his people strength and peace. Both verses illustrate the way God "settles us down" in our thinking and our feelings and gives us a quiet, inner confidence that he is in control. When we know this, deep inside, we enjoy the good times more and are able to persevere through the tough times. Jeremiah's statement summarizes it well: "But blessed is the man who trusts in the LORD, whose confidence is in him" (Jeremiah 17:7).

Even if these were God's only blessings, they would be worth any price.

Spiritual Blessings

This third area of blessing is one that most Christians believe with their minds but struggle to receive in their hearts. It's the blessing of grace. Looking back through all the verses about blessings, one passage that sparked my memory was Romans 4:7-8: "Blessed are they whose transgressions are forgiven, whose sins are covered. Blessed is the man whose sin the Lord will never count against him."

As a freshman at a Christian college, I was reading this verse one day and this phrase, "Blessed is the man whose sin the Lord will never count against him," grabbed me. Wait a minute, I thought! That can't be an accurate translation. Even though I knew God forgave sin, I always thought you had to "walk the straight and narrow" path or else. I was a pretty smug Christian, actually, because I worked hard on my behavior, my influence, my doctrine, and so forth. That was how I would *stay* forgiven. And, if I slipped up once in a while, I knew I should repent, ask forgiveness, and quit it. So, when the impact of the verse hit me I was offended.

The New International Version, was then only a couple of years old, and I thought it must be a loose translation to claim that it was possible to have such a relationship with God that he didn't even count it when I sinned. "Surely God isn't that easy," I thought. So I looked at the King James Version. It surprised me too. It says, "Blessed is the man to whom the Lord will not impute sin." I knew imputed had something to do with "charge against," and it sounded like a verse that challenged my whole theology about how to be "right" before God. So, partly out of self-defense and partly out of curiosity, I asked an upperclassman in my dorm, who was also a biblical languages major, to look at this passage in the Greek New Testament and tell me what it *really* said.

To my amazement, he told me it literally meant what the NIV said! This started me on a path toward the reality of knowing God truly as a God of grace (Romans 5:2), believing that Jesus' blood continually purifies me from all sin (1 John 1:7), and feeling that I am deeply loved, no matter what (2 Thessalonians 2:16-17).

When we fall or fail, we start over, knowing God will help us. This truth brings spiritual liberty and freedom to those who follow God by changing our desires. God doesn't require us to earn our blessing, yet he does want us to know that we can miss a blessing through disobedience. That's why, in Malachi 3:9, he said the whole nation of Israel was "under a curse." God's love is unconditional, but many of his blessings are not—they are conditional on our decisions and follow through. Our repentance gives us the privilege of standing under the overwhelming flow of blessings.

This is what God wanted to prove to Israel. By not giving "the tenth" back to the Lord (Leviticus 27:30, 32), they had robbed him and themselves. Why would God use such a strong word here? Why did he accuse Israel of stealing from him? I think God wanted to get their attention.

The same is true for us today. When we don't give at least 10 percent of our income, God will want to get our attention too. Since he owns everything, the real issue is not about giving 10 percent, it's about managing the entire 100 percent. Do we think it is ours or his? Committing to tithe helps us remember that it's all his. Once we settle that thought firmly and finally, it positions our hearts, minds, and lives to receive enormous blessings.

Some Christians question the present validity of God's promise to pour out a blessing. They argue that since the Book of Malachi is in the Old Testament it refers to people who were under the law of Moses. They then conclude that Christians are not required to tithe. Whenever I hear Christians challenge this passage, I ask them to reconsider. Instead of asking, "Do I have to tithe?" ask, "Do I want to be blessed?" Has God stopped blessing us as a direct result of our lack of financial giving to support Kingdom work? Consider what the apostle Paul wrote in 2 Corinthians 9:6-11:

> Remember this: Whoever sows sparingly will also reap sparingly, and whoever sows generously will also

reap generously. Each man should give what he has decided in his heart to give, not reluctantly or under compulsion, for God loves a cheerful giver. And God is able to make all grace abound to you, so that in all things at all times, having all that you need, you will abound in every good work. Now he who supplies seed to the sower and bread for food will also supply and increase your store of seed and will enlarge the harvest of your righteousness. You will be made rich in every way so that you can be generous on every occasion, and through us your generosity will result in thanksgiving to God.

The context is a financial context. He is not simply referring to spiritual blessings. The seed here clearly refers to physical resources that allow good work to be done. And God promises to "increase your store of seed" so that more good can be done.

In reality, the price God wants us to pay in order to receive blessing is not money. Giving money is not the point. It's merely an application of the point. The point is our faith. The real question Christians should ask in reference to tithing is: Do I have faith in God to provide more for me after I give?

Because of writing *Take God at His Word*, I've heard first-hand accounts of surprising ways God has responded when people tithed. For example, I know of many people who made financial commitments to tithe or give special offerings who weren't sure how they would be able to follow through on the decision. Within a few days they learned how God provided for them in remarkable ways: new jobs, surprise raises in salary or commissions, and unexpected insurance checks or IRS refunds. One elderly lady received notice that her Social Security benefits were being increased. A single mom found out that her son earned a basketball scholarship as a walk-on player! A minister friend was told that his sizable school debt had been forgiven. A businessman was issued some valuable stock options. It's an exciting list that keeps growing!

God will not guarantee a specific financial result, because he is sovereign. He doesn't present himself as some type of heavenly vending machine giving everyone a tenfold increase in their money. That kind of predictability would tempt us to trade our obedience for a return-on-investment formula. It is always foolish to try to put God in a box. But the one common denominator I sensed from each of the people I've heard from is that they simply *knew* in their hearts that this was how God responded to their faith. Far more important than the financial advantage of the blessing was the tangible confirmation that God was presently and personally active in their lives. Now that's a priceless blessing!

So remember, God longs to bless you. He wants to prove how faithful and powerful he is to those who trust him. Instead of worrying about how much you might need to increase your giving, begin looking for how God will come through. His response may surprise you!

Let God Prove That He Wants to Protect You from a Curse

Two words hit pretty hard in Malachi 3: "rob" and "curse." We've already looked at why God used the word *rob* to get our attention. Now let's examine why he warns about a curse.

In the Bible the word *curse* is typically used to describe the opposite affect of blessing. So, if blessing from God refers to the good things God brings or allows to come into our lives, curse refers to the penalties that come from disobedience.

Here's another powerful passage:

Deuteronomy 30:19-20
This day I call heaven and earth as witnesses against you that I have set before you life and death, blessings and curses. Now choose life, so that you and your children may live and that you may love the LORD your God, listen to his voice, and hold fast to him. For the LORD is your life, and he will give you many years in the land he swore to give to your fathers, Abraham, Isaac and Jacob.

Following God leads to life and is full of blessings. Rejecting God leads to death and carries the consequences of ignoring or disobeying God. That's why the Bible uses the word "curse" or "curses." It's not a magical incantation like we hear about in books and movies. It's a reference to what God will cause or allow to occur if the path of blessing is not taken.

Other passages which make this clear include:

Deuteronomy 28:20
The LORD will send on you curses, confusion and rebuke in everything you put your hand to, until you are destroyed and come to sudden ruin because of the evil you have done in forsaking him.

Proverbs 3:33
The LORD's curse is on the house of the wicked, but he

blesses the home of the righteous.

Proverbs 28:27
He who gives to the poor will lack nothing, but he who closes his eyes to them receives many curses.

Jeremiah 17:5
This is what the LORD says: "Cursed is the one who trusts in man, who depends on flesh for his strength and whose heart turns away from the LORD."

As a penalty for what happened in the Garden of Eden, God cursed the serpent (Genesis 3:14). He also cursed the ground Adam would farm (Genesis 3:17) indicating that work and life would become hard and painful outside the garden. If Adam had realized that his place of blessing was near God and the tree of life, perhaps he would have resisted the temptation to take from the tree of the knowledge of good and evil. Even from the beginning of time the issue of blessing and curses is related to trusting and relying on God.

God also promised to bless the people who blessed Abraham and curse those who cursed him (Genesis 12:3). God was saying he would bring good consequences on those who helped Abraham and bad consequences on those who opposed him. This promise came true a number of times, with Pharaoh (Genesis 12:17), at Sodom and Gomorrah (Genesis 19:29), and with Abimelech (Genesis 20:3, 17).

It Can Happen Today

Malachi 3 lists some of the bad consequences God wanted Israel to avoid. He wanted to prevent pests from devouring their crops and the premature dropping of fruit from the vines (verse 11). This agricultural example has many parallels today even for people who aren't farmers. If you're in business, this could mean God will keep you from losing an important account. If you're a factory worker, the parallel could be that you won't be passed over unfairly for a promotion. Or, if you're an hourly worker, maybe it means you'll not get bumped off the schedule for overtime. If you're a server in a restaurant, maybe it means fewer people short you on tips. If you're a schoolteacher, maybe it means you'll have parents who are supportive of the children in your class (my wife is a teacher so she really likes this example). Do you get the point? Look at your life situation. Are you pleased or disappointed with your employment and income situations? If hardship is the rule of the day for you, have you considered the possibility that you haven't put God first in tithes and offerings?

God's remedy for the effects of the curse is for a person to simply return to him (verse 7). He longs to rescue us from this dilemma. Returning to God and receiving his blessing is true in giving. It's true in our devotion to him. It's true in salvation. He doesn't ask us to prove we're worth the effort. He doesn't require us to "pay back" what we've failed to give him. While I recommend righting any previous wrongs, God doesn't have some "improvement threshold" that means we must earn our way back into his good graces. The action God looks for is simple: Return to him. In giving, this means to trust his provision, his faithfulness, and his power enough to begin tithing or increasing our giving by adding special offerings to support good works.

Verse 12 continues: "'Then all the nations will call

you blessed, for yours will be a delightful land,' says the LORD Almighty." This is God's way of saying he doesn't want to have to punish us any longer than is necessary. He wants "the nations," the unbelieving world, to see that God's people are blessed. He wants our lives to be described as a delight. Let God prove it to you!

You Do Make a Difference

When Israel failed to tithe, the temple storehouse was empty of the crops people were to give to God. In ancient times, people made offerings of gold and silver, clothing, and other materials. But they also gave at least 10 percent of their crops, for these crops were used to provide for the needs of the priests and the poor. In other words, their gifts were used to support ministry.

This is another reason why this passage has such practical application today. When you and I tithe into the storehouse of the church (1 Corinthians 16:1-2), we are releasing funds into the care of godly leaders who will use these resources to support ministry and ministry activities. Every gift mattered then and still matters. Every research study I've looked at for the past twenty years indicates that on the average, Christians give about 2.5 percent of their income to the Lord's work. Any amount that is given is important, but can you imagine the impact of four times the amount of money if every Christian gave at least 10 percent of their income to the Lord? So much ministry would be going on that the world would sit up and take notice. We could support more missionaries, provide for the unemployed and the poor. We could unleash endless creative ideas for new ministries. One study calculated that if all the church members in America lost their jobs and tithed from their welfare payments, contributions would rise by 35 percent.[1]

That's amazing, isn't it? What this passage also implies to me is that God wants to create a "culture of generosity." Tithing is really a standard we need to jump over. One minister told me that his congregation responded so well to *Take God at His Word* because they were "hungry for a standard." Usually, we know we should give to God but are unsure where to start. If we don't start by stretching, we'll have a hard time growing and excelling in this important part of our Christian life. Since God owns everything and can create anything, it's clear that he doesn't ask us to give because he needs it. God asks us to give because *we* need it. We need to become generous people because it loosens up stingy attitudes in our hearts. When we become more generous with our checkbook, it will encourage us to be more generous in the way we treat others. A friend commented that he applied this principle beyond his tithes and offerings to God and had started using "tipping" in a restaurant as a way to encourage a more generous attitude. He said his wife used to be a waitress and she always hated working on Sundays. First, she missed the opportunity to worship and fellowship, and second she said the Christians she served seldom tipped very well, if at all. Often the difference between a good tip and bad tip was only a dollar. Initially, his desire to become more sensitive to the needs and concerns of others motivated his generosity in tipping. He now also sees it as a way to leave his server with a better impression of Christians. His example has encouraged me, as well. As Jesus said, "In the same way, let your light shine before men, that they may see your good deeds and praise your Father in heaven" (Matthew 5:16).

Notes:
[1] Robert Jeffress, *Guilt-Free Living* (Wheaton: Tyndale House Publishers, 1996).

Think It Through
Let Me Prove It to You

1. Since God invites you to "put him to the test" in tithing, what stories could you tell others about this step of faith?

2. What blessings do you need from God right now? Do you have a curse you would like removed? Ask God about these.

3. Of the four areas of blessing listed below, where do you feel the strongest? Which one stretches you the most?

   Loyalty to God
   Physical and material provision
   Emotional well-being
   Spiritual wealth

4. How do you think the Lord wants you to put this chapter's teaching into practice?

Command those who are rich in this present world not to be arrogant nor to put their hope in wealth, which is so uncertain, but to put their hope in God, who richly provides us with everything for our enjoyment. Command them to do good, to be rich in good deeds, and to be generous and willing to share. In this way they will lay up treasure for themselves as a firm foundation for the coming age, so that they may take hold of the life that is truly life.

1 Timothy 6:17-19

Let's Pray

Lord, you are the Source of true life. Thank you for giving me the opportunity, as your Word says, to "take hold of true life." I am eager to rest in the confidence that comes from a closer walk with you. I am thankful for all you do and will do. And I'm thankful for the events and circumstances that have led me to this place in my life. Please bless me with greater contentment and help me sense that my security is found only in you. Through Jesus I pray. Amen.

CHAPTER THREE:
Take Hold of True Life

I'm fascinated by the wild success of the television program "Who Wants to Be a Millionaire?" Contestants have a shot at winning a million dollars if they can answer enough trivia questions from Regis to pile up the big bucks. Millions of viewers watch each episode with excitement. Suspense builds as the audience pulls for the contestant in the hot seat to win the jackpot. When the poor soul misses the answer, everyone shouts at their TV, "I knew that!" Actually, very few people win the big prize, but the mere possibility keeps drawing big ratings numbers.

I believe God wants to make us millionaires, too—although not necessarily in our bank accounts. What he wants to do is to make us millionaires in "true life." Paul told Timothy:

Command those who are rich in this present world not to be arrogant nor to put their hope in wealth, which is so uncertain, but to put their hope in

God, who richly provides us with everything for our enjoyment. Command them to do good, to be rich in good deeds, and to be generous and willing to share. In this way they will lay up treasure for themselves as a firm foundation for the coming age, so that they may take hold of the life that is truly life.

(1 Timothy 6:17-19)

When You Have "True Life" You're Truly Rich!

God is more than capable of showering us with enumerable physical and financial resources. Yet, what he ultimately wants to do is to make us rich in the more valuable areas of our life. The Lord demonstrates his concern about accomplishing this in us by inspiring Paul to tell Timothy in verse 17 that he should command his listeners about these matters. Some translations say "Charge them..." And I'm sure it had nothing to do with using credit cards! The grammar in this verse is quite strong in English, yet it's even stronger in the Greek language of the New Testament. A literal translation would read, "Continue to charge them..." or "Keep on commanding them..." The point God makes is: We will always need instruction and encouragement on this issue. Money is an important tool for doing good but it can also seduce us to place our trust in possessions and the pursuit of greater wealth. True life is much different and much better!

True Life Opens the Door for Wisdom

It's one thing to have money. It's an entirely different thing to know how to use it wisely. God's wisdom says, "Don't put your hope in worldly wealth." Some of the reasons are spelled out clearly in this passage. First, worldly wealth can make you arrogant. Paul's word for arrogant in verse 17 means "high minded." Have you ever noticed how some rich people give the impression that they are above others? Some even look down on those who have less. Financial pride often leads to a big fall from the lofty summit. It doesn't matter if you're a leader on Wall Street or a supervisor on an assembly line, just because you might make more money than someone, it doesn't mean you're worth more. Jesus proved this long ago. No one was worth more by either heaven's or the world's standards than the Lord, yet Paul writes,

> Your attitude should be the same as
> that of Christ Jesus:
> Who, being in very nature God,
>   did not consider equality with God
>   something to be grasped,
> but made himself nothing,
>   taking the very nature of a
>   servant,
>   being made in human likeness.
> And being found in appearance as a
>   man,
> he humbled himself
> and became obedient to death—
>   even death on a cross!
> Therefore God exalted him to the
>   highest place
> and gave him the name that is above
>   every name.
>
> (Philippians 2:5-9)

It's much wiser to be humble than to be arrogant. People will be able to both appreciate and look up to you, only in the right way.

You shouldn't put your hope in worldly wealth for a second reason—it is incredibly uncertain. It is amazing to see how easily we can fall into the trap of thinking financial wealth is a sure thing. Early in 2000 many economic camps circulated glowing reports and forecasts about the stock market opportunities. Millions of novice investors brought billions of dollars into aggressive mutual funds and risky start-up investments. "Playing it safe" was thought to be an unwise strategy in the greatest Bull market in the history of the world. A few cautious souls warned that the "bubble would surely burst" at some time but their warnings were drowned out by a sea of television shows, newspaper stories, and magazine articles touting the potential of companies that had never even turned a dime's worth of profit. Many investors hurried to get in on the latest IPO so they could "ride a stock up" planning to sell it for a tidy profit. It was a heady time for many in the financial world. Many Christians spoke of doing the same thing, too.

But midway through the year, the bubble did burst. Tech stocks dropped like a rock. Internet firms that once advertised during the Super Bowl closed their doors only a few months later. A new president was elected and even his supporters wondered if the economy might go into recession, leaving him to blame for an economic downturn that he had no part in creating. As I write this book, no self-respecting financial "expert" will boast that he or she is certain about anything except that times are uncertain! It's easy to see how even though 1 Timothy

6:17-19 was written nearly 2,000 years ago, it reads like today's news.

Recently, I was reading an article in the *Wall Street Journal*. The headline read, "Indexes Disagree over Odds for Recession." The writer's story drove home this point. "Not only are lots of economists confused about where the economy is headed, but the two indexes often used to predict economic activity currently offer exasperatingly different outlooks."[1]

Why do we ever become convinced that worldly wealth is a sure thing? We should never trust in anyone but God and in anything but his provision. Companies fail, jobs are eliminated, the stock market goes up and down. No one can predict these fluctuations. But God is still sovereign. He is the source of all blessing to the Christian.

A third problem with worldly wealth is that it can be dangerous. Just a few verses earlier (6:9-10) Paul wrote that the desire to get rich causes temptation to do things that aren't very wise. Most Americans overspend and undersave. Then, when money is needed to cover an emergency expense, pay for a truly needed item, or even give to support an important cause, the resources have already been drained. That's why Paul calls this desire a "trap." It's not that money is a trap. Money is only a tool, like time, intelligence, or other resources. But when the desire to possess worldly wealth overshoots our ability to handle it, we will fall into situations that imprison us. Paul may even have a sequence for us in these verses. The desire to get rich creates a vulnerability to temptation, which sets a trap, which pitches us into unchecked desires that lead to our downfall.

Notice in verse 10 that he mentions "some . . . people have wandered from the faith." Financial wisdom has spiritual as well as physical implications.

On the other hand, you'll be a millionaire in wisdom if you put your hope in God. Wealth is uncertain. God is certain. It impresses me that Paul said to put hope *in* God. He is a person more than a financial plan. When you think about stewardship, do you think it's a philosophy for giving? Or do you think that putting your confidence in your financial skills is being wise, prudent, and prepared? While there is truth in godly stewardship and conservative spending decisions, the wisest human thinking is no substitute for childlike trust in God. This passage calls God a provider. He didn't merely create the world and walk away. He created the world, and our lives, with a view to providing what we need to live on and share with others. Plus, this passage says God also provides us with everything for *our enjoyment*. Isn't this one of the most exciting phrases in the Bible? God wants his children to enjoy life. Where did we get the idea that God doesn't want us to have fun, relax, and experience pleasure? Certainly not from the Bible! Take a look at these verses and see how God wants us to enjoy

Your job and possessions (Ecclesiastes 5:19)
What we build with our hands (Isaiah 65:22)
Peace and security (Jeremiah 33:6)
Food (Acts 14:17)
Health (3 John 2)

Other passages speak of enjoying the Lord's protection (Psalm 5:11), his abundant goodness in our lives (Psalm 126:3; 145:7), and the ability to live, at all times with a sense of joy that comes from the presence of God's Spirit in our lives (Romans 15:13).

What God actually says about enjoyment and what we may *think* he says about it can be vastly different. He wants to be in the center of our lives so that enjoyment can come as a by-product of his presence within us. If enjoyment is the focus, we'll wind up in the same mess as Solomon: "Whoever loves money never has money enough; whoever loves wealth is never satisfied with his income. This too is meaningless" (Ecclesiastes 5:10).

The ultimate issue is: What is my priority? If it is God, I can relax and know that he is in control and will guide my steps. He will give me wisdom about spending, saving, giving, investing, and preparing for the future.

True Life Cultivates Contentment

First Timothy 6:17 also makes it clear that God gives us everything. Living by faith that God will meet all your needs is fundamental to taking God at his word. The Bible says he *richly* provides. This word refers to abundance. It means God is not a miser in the way he provides. We've already seen this truth in the first chapter, but here is where I want to take this principle a step further. God will meet our needs and give us the ability to share so he can teach us contentment. Contentment is the secret to financial happiness.

Contentment comes when you trust God to give you what you can handle financially. If you feel you need an increased supply of finances, then let God train you. There are a number of reasons why God might have a tight hold on your financial reins. If you will trust him to stay in control of the training process, you'll be much better off. Remember, he is interested in your good.

God's Four-Session Training Course

Training Session 1—Maturity. Everyone has friends or loved ones who have suffered in the long run from receiving too much income too quickly. It makes sense that God loves you enough to protect you from this trap, if you'll let him. Make some wise, mature, firm decisions about how you'll handle increased financial wealth when it comes. Pray about and make fresh new decisions about your spending, savings, and giving levels. Then submit these decisions to the Lord, follow through with them and wait. This may be what God is looking for in your life.

Training Session 2—Timing. You may be prepared for a change in your financial trustworthiness, and all that remains is God's perfect timing to fit all the other pieces in place. Most financial conditions include a number of variables. Like the individual situations of the people in your life, pending circumstances, and your life experiences, to list a few. It's usually hard to understand timing issues before the fact. It's afterwards, in retrospect, that we can fully see how God was orchestrating events, details, and the hearts of others to create a wonderful outcome. Many times we recognize that the results would not have been as good if things had worked more quickly, the way we wanted, or prayed for. I think it is God in control—"providence."

Training Session 3—Discipline. Perhaps we have made unwise or destructive financial decisions. Even though we may have repented of them, God still allows the consequences of these decisions to follow us. He does this to teach us at both a heart and head level so that we will truly learn to let go of the dangerous path and grab hold of him and his good path for our lives. It works best when we repent of the bad decisions as soon as we recognize them. True repentance breaks the devil's hold on our hearts, even though we may not receive immediate or complete relief from the struggle or financial hardship. In the process of working through the discipline, he affords us time to learn valuable money management skills and even more valuable money management attitudes. The difficulties of discipline create memories that protect us from future mistakes. Without the pain we would almost certainly forget and repeat the same mistakes.

Training Session 4—Testing. This session is completely positive. God may be using the "lean times" in your finances to build your faith. The bigger the test, the greater faith becomes. Since God has linked our heart to our treasure (Matthew 6:21), he often uses financial tests to expand our willingness to trust him with greater responsibility. In Jesus' parable about the shrewd manager, he said, "Whoever can be trusted with very little can also be trusted with much, and whoever is dishonest with very little will also be dishonest with much. So if you have not been trustworthy in handling worldly wealth, who will trust you with true riches?" (Luke 16:10-11).

Obviously, when we use a small amout of money carefully and in a godly way, we are learning to be "trusted with very little." Jesus said that the faithful management of worldly wealth will enable us to handle "true riches." What are true riches? Jesus didn't tell us specifically, but it must be tremendous. Perhaps it refers to God granting us greater effectiveness in ministry, or a better understanding of his ways, or even a clearer realization of how much he loves us. Whatever the details, true riches must be great—and worth the wait.

So, whether it's one of these training sessions or others, the first step to financial contentment is trusting God to know what we are ready for, and being ready to learn how we can handle more. He wants to trust us, but we need to be ready.

The second step to contentment flows out of the first one. By learning to trust the Lord with our present financial situation, and believing that he knows and cares about us, we focus on enjoying what we *have*. First Timothy 6:17 says God richly provides. No matter what our current level of need (or perceived need), God always provides richly for us. Not only that, his purpose in providing is not just so we have just barely enough to scrape by, but that we have enough to enjoy, as well. Once you believe God has provided things for you to enjoy, recognize them and enjoy them.

My economics professor in college, Dr. Don Diffine, has written an excellent booklet entitled, *Good News: The Bad News Is Wrong*. Dr. Diffine points out several ways the vast majority of Americans are better off than they were a hundred years ago. For example,

> A recent report from the Cato Institute described some of the nonmedical ways in which our lives have changed since 1900: "An analysis of almost every indicator of health, welfare, safety, environmental quality and social conditions reveals great progress. Even the poorest Americans today enjoy conveniences that millionaires never dreamed possible 100 years ago."[2]

A Golden Age?

Here are just a few of their observations, compared with a century ago in America:

• Four times as many adults are getting their high school degrees.

• Six times as many women now have bachelor's degrees.

• Nearly all American homes (98 percent) have telephones, electricity, and a flush toilet.

• Accidental deaths have dropped by 61 percent despite all the additional cars and airplanes and the millions of people using them.

• Manufacturing wages are four times higher.

• Household assets are seven times greater.

• More than 70 percent of Americans have at least one automobile, a VCR, a microwave oven, air conditioning, cable television, a washer and dryer— all things that many of us tend to take for granted.

• The average workweek is 30 percent shorter (thirty-five hours now versus fifty hours a week in 1909).

• We are spending twice as much time in leisure activities as our forebearers did in 1900.[3]

Reading this list of blessings and benefits causes me to remember how much I have to enjoy. If we fail to realize and enjoy what we now have, we set ourselves up for the devil to con us into requiring more than we need.

In the last few years I've learned to pause long enough to appreciate something that I used to take for granted.

I frequently find myself looking at the beautiful morning sky on my drive to work thinking, "God, you sure made a pretty morning." My enjoyment has increased by the mere realization of these things: driving in an air conditioned car, picking up the phone to call my parents, and being able to pay my son's baseball fee and then help coach his team. I've learned to better enjoy eating at a restaurant, going to the mall, and simply buying a pair of shoes. In short, I believe God is helping me avoid taking so many things for granted. It also seems as though he is frequently reminding me to see that technology and modern conveniences are not "my right." They are not necessities. They are not absolutes.

Much of the stress I face in modern life is due to having more rather than less. Here's another illustration comparing modern Western life with life in a third world nation. Imagine you were immediately whisked from your current home and became the citizen of a country that has very little. Here's what your life would be like.

9 Steps to Third World Living

• First, take out the furniture: leave a few old blankets, a kitchen table, maybe a wooden chair. You've never had a bed, remember?

• Second, throw out your clothes. Each person in the family may keep the oldest suit or dress, a shirt or blouse. The head of the family has the only pair of shoes.

• Third, all kitchen appliances have vanished.

Keep a box of matches, a small bag of flour, some sugar and salt, a handful of onions, a dish of dried beans. Rescue the moldy potatoes from the garbage can: those are tonight's meal.

- Fourth, dismantle the bathroom, shut off the running water, take out the wiring and the lights and everything that runs by electricity

- Fifth, take away the house and move the family into the toolshed.

- Sixth, no more postman, fireman, government services. The two-classroom school is three miles away, but only two of your seven children attend anyway, and they walk.

- Seventh, throw out your bankbooks, stock certificates, pension plans, insurance policies. You now have a cash hoard of $5.

- Eighth, get out and start cultivating your three acres. Try hard to raise $300 in cash crops because your landlord wants one third and your moneylender 10 percent.

- Ninth, find some way for your children to bring in a little extra money so you have something to eat most days. But it won't be enough to keep bodies healthy—so lop off 25 to 30 years of life.[4]

Taking stock of these realities is not meant as a put down to any one else's culture. Nor is it meant to minimize the hardship of a particular group or person struggling with a scarcity of the resources most of us take for granted. Rather it is meant to give an encouraging perspective. God has given so many things for our enjoyment: modern conveniences such as electric lights, automobiles, air conditioning, running water, telephones, grocery stores, and more. Add your own list. Thank God more frequently for the privileges you have. A good friend and I have shared many meals in a restaurant. Without exception, he prays, "God, we thank you that we have choices about what we eat." The first time I heard him pray that I felt so humbled. I always pray before meals, but I seldom thought about what a blessing it is to order from a bountiful menu, and have someone bring it to me (and clean up after me!).

Paying more attention to what you have received gives God the credit. The Bible says, "But the wisdom that comes from heaven is first of all pure; then peace-loving, considerate, submissive, full of mercy and good fruit, impartial and sincere" (James 3:17). So, like our jobs (Deuteronomy 8:18) and our very lives (Acts 17:28), enjoy the daily resources God provides. Take pleasure in a child's giggle, a beautiful sunrise, and loving friends. Giving special attention to these blessings will open the door to many others you may be taking for granted. You'll experience much more true life.

True Life Intensifies Generosity

First Timothy 6:18 tells us that to be truly generous there are three actions we should give attention to:
1. Good works—"to do good, to be rich in good deeds"
2. Giving resources—"to be generous"
3. Being "willing to share"

The first one is serving others daily, and it refers to

the pattern of service that God wants as the character of our lives. Jesus put it this way, "In the same way, let your light shine before men, that they may see your good deeds and praise your Father in heaven" (Matthew 5:16). We can find so many places to serve. There are people around us every day who need help, encouragement, and love.

The second action is giving our resources to God. The King James Version translates this phrase, "ready to distribute." It means, literally, "good at giving something." In Luke 3:11 it describes someone with two coats sharing with another who has none. It's also found in Romans 12:8 during the teaching about spiritual gifts and says giving should be done "with liberality" (NKJV). Ephesians 4:28 discusses our need to work for a living so that we will have resources to share with someone in need. It's clear that God wants us to willingly turn loose of physical resources in order to help others. This is a reason why I believe so strongly in the importance of taking up an offering each week. The best example of this is 1 Corinthians 16:1-2, "Now about the collection for God's people: Do what I told the Galatian churches to do. On the first day of every week, each one of you should set aside a sum of money in keeping with his income, saving it up, so that when I come no collections will have to be made." From this passage we learn four wise principles about giving money to do God's work.

Principle 1—Give Regularly

Paul said they should give money "every week." I take this to mean I should give each Sunday and at other times, as well, when a special need is presented. The discipline of regular giving holds me accountable and allows me to give a lot more over the long haul.

Principle 2—Give Personally

The Bible says, "each one of you." When our children were old enough to begin to participate in the worship service at church, my wife and I gave them money to put in the offering plate or basket. Now they're growing up to appreciate this aspect of their Christian life. I believe they see giving as an act of worship to the Lord, too. Another wonderful blessing of giving has been seeing my teenage daughter raise funds for a mission trip to help teach orphans in Russia about Jesus and his love. It's been easy for her to ask for support because she has grown up giving to support the Lord's work. I can recall giving from my early childhood because when I was very young, my parents gave me money to put in the collection plate. As I grew up, I gave part of my allowance back to the Lord, then later on gave from my income when I worked a part-time job at Dairy Queen in high school. Those patterns of giving have become healthy giving habits. The Lord has taken great care of me, and I am certain that he has used these funds to do more good than I may ever know in this life.

Principle 3—Give Systematically

This part of the instruction says to "set aside a sum of money." When we "set aside" money on a regular basis we are being systematic. This lets us think through the need and our response. It's not a haphazard or casual approach. It's true ministry. Plus, the more we as individuals commit to being systematic and predictable in our giving, the easier it will be for church leaders to determine where funds should be spent.

In this passage the Corinthian church was collecting funds for Paul to take to the poor Christians in Jerusalem. Even though this was a special circumstance, the giving game plan is a practical one for today. The only difference is in size and complexity. The real question for giving to the local ministry of a church is twofold: Is the money given to the Lord? And is the work helping to preach the gospel or support ministry efforts to better establish the kingdom of Jesus (Acts 14:22)? Systematic giving is actually an extension of "regular giving." Regular giving does more good for the kingdom because it increases the total amount given. Systematic giving causes us to plan our giving and target funds based on our God-given income.

Principle 4—Give Proportionally

The age-old question Christians ask is, How much should I give? While no specific amount is mandated in the New Testament, this verse indicates it should somehow be linked to a person's income. The word here literally means, "as prospered." Practically speaking, I apply this by targeting a percentage of our total income and give it back to God. The starting percentage, as you know from chapter 2 is 10 percent, but why think of 10 percent as the end? Several situations could and should cause you to raise this amount:

- When your income increases beyond your needs, consider adding a higher percentage of the increase. See what God does next.

- When there is a special need, make sacrificial gifts and offerings beyond the tithes. This could be building projects, mission efforts, or benevolence needs.

• When you have an unexpected "windfall," consider giving half or maybe all of it back to the Lord.

• When you're in a tight situation, or if your income drops unexpectedly and you aren't sure how you can keep giving at your previous level, don't back off. Give God an opportunity to surprise you with his protection, as well as his provision. You may find you need less to live on than you thought. Simplifying your lifestyle and reducing your expenses might turn out to be a bigger blessing than having a higher income. I've known many people who would attest to that statement. Commit to give from your monetary resources in addition to your time and effort.

When I was just a "cub preacher" one of the wise, old members at my congregation told me, "Hood, don't work harder. Work smarter." Actually, I've tried to do both. Giving regularly, personally, systematically, and proportionately is working harder and smarter *for the Lord*! Our whole-hearted commitment to this kind of generosity will surely lead to more seed being sown and a greater harvest of righteousness coming as a result (2 Corinthians 9:10).

The third action of generosity is being willing to share. Did you know your willingness to open your heart shows you have people concerns high on your priority list? The word "share" in this verse is a form of the word for fellowship, *koinonia*. God is saying "Be willing to invest your life in the lives of others." How Christlike is it when we say we serve God and give money to accomplish his work, yet remain passive and distant toward people, their hurts and pains? Our generosity is a powerful expression of our Christ like compassion.

True Life Prepares Us for Eternal Life

The end result of this teaching from Paul is to focus us on our true home: heaven. Everything we do to restore godliness to our finances in order to help others is preparation for the "coming age." The good we do, the money we give, the people we care for are all "treasure" in their own right. And by investing this treasure with God, we have access to more and more of His riches. This is not only for the future, either. It's for today. As the apostle Paul says, doing this will allow us to "take hold" or "seize" *true life.*

Notes:

[1] *Wall Street Journal* (April 17, 2001) AZ. Used by permission.
[2] Don Diffine, *Good News: The Bad News Is Wrong* (Searcy: Harding University, Beldon Center for Private Enterprise Education, January 2001). Used by permission.
[3] Diffine.
[4] From "12 Steps to Third World Living," IC #26 (Context Institute, Summer 1990), 7.

Think It Through
Take Hold of True Life

1. In this chapter we heard God say, "Take hold of true life." In your view, what does "true life" include? What do you think keeps people from seizing this reality?

2. What do you consider to be the keys to contentment?

3. If "being rich in good deeds" is one of God's measures for true wealth, how rich are you?

   Poorhouse   Getting by   Average   Blessed   Millionaire

4. How do you think the Lord wants you to put this chapter's teaching into practice?

CHAPTER THREE

But the one who received the seed that fell on good soil is the man who hears the word and understands it. He produces a crop, yielding a hundred, sixty or thirty times what was sown.

Matthew 13:23

Let's Pray

Almighty God, thank you for telling me to "expect a harvest!" I am looking forward to learning how to better listen to you and follow through with the direction you give me. Lord, I am not just interested in learning this lesson in my giving, but also in my entire life. I do not want any area of my life to escape your patient, wise, blessed instruction. I am truly looking for a harvest in every part of my life and the lives of my loved ones. Thank you for making this possible. Thank you for not leaving me to fend for myself in a demanding world of pressure, stress, and struggle. You raise me above all this because you are a God who can do the impossible. Thank you now for the harvests you will grant me. In Jesus' name. Amen.

CHAPTER FOUR:
Expect a Harvest

God has packed another exciting message into one of the most familiar parables: the parable of the soils. What's surprising to me is that I've never heard this parable used to deal with the subject of money before. But it's a perfect fit.

Then he told them many things in parables, saying: "A farmer went out to sow his seed. As he was scattering the seed, some fell along the path, and the birds came and ate it up. Some fell on rocky places, where it did not have much soil. It sprang up quickly, because the soil was shallow. But when the sun came up, the plants were scorched, and they withered because they had no root. Other seed fell among thorns, which grew up and choked the plants. Still other seed fell on good soil, where it produced a crop—a hundred, sixty or thirty times what was sown. He who has ears, let him hear.

Listen then to what the parable of the sower means: When anyone hears the message about the kingdom and does not understand it, the evil one comes and snatches away what was sown in his heart. This is the seed sown along the path. The one who received the seed that fell on rocky places is the man who hears the word and at once receives it with joy. But since he has no root, he lasts only a short time. When trouble or persecution comes because of the word, he quickly falls away. The one who received the seed that fell among the thorns is the man who hears the word, but the worries of this life and the deceitfulness of wealth choke it, making it unfruitful. But the one who received the seed that fell on good soil is the man who hears the word and understands it. He produces a crop, yielding a hundred, sixty or thirty times what was sown."

(Matthew 13:3-9, 18-23)

When Jesus told this parable he was speaking to large crowds and teaching them about crucial Kingdom principles for life. Matthew 13 actually contains seven Kingdom parables, so it's clear that a lot of good stuff is packed into this short section of Scripture but I had never spotted the link between giving and the parable of the soils until recently. While reading the Gospel of Matthew, I came to this section of Scripture and was greatly tempted to skim it since I had read and preached this story so many times. I thought I knew it through and through!

However something unusual happened as I read the story again. I had been praying for new insights to extend the teaching for this series, but I wasn't thinking about this desire while reading Matthew 13 again that day. When I read verse 23, my heart almost stopped, "But the one who received the seed that fell on good soil is the man who hears the word and understands it. He produces a crop, yielding a hundred, sixty or thirty times what was sown." It dawned on me this was yet another teaching on giving and expecting a harvest from the Lord!

I hurriedly grabbed a pen and paper and went back through the entire story. In less than five minutes I outlined a new lesson with a fresh perspective on how God prepares us for big things when we continue to give generously.

If we apply these action steps, we can expect an exciting harvest from God. Their impact will ultimately affect all areas of our lives and reach into our families, our congregations, our communities, and around the world.

Understand with Your Heart

When the disciples first heard this parable, they were baffled about its meaning and even more clueless about how to apply it. So Jesus explains it to them step by step. "When anyone hears the message about the kingdom and does not understand it, the evil one comes and snatches away what was sown in his heart. This is the seed sown along the path" (Matthew 13:19).

This parable is first and foremost about how we receive spiritual truth. In fact, while the application I'm drawing for this chapter is specifically targeted toward giving, we could take the same action steps I'll share and reapply them to other areas of life—marriage, parenting, sharing our faith, building a Christian business, being salt and light in our neighborhood, and many other important issues and needs.

Jesus says the evil one tries to steal messages about the Kingdom. He doesn't do this by messing with our minds, he messes with our hearts. We think we understand only with our minds, but Jesus says we must understand with our hearts.

The way we hear determines how we will respond, and the way we respond determines how much we reap in the Kingdom area we're learning about.

This is why we can listen to all kinds of sermons on just about every subject, agree with the logic, reasoning, and application but never change our behavior. It's because we never understood with our hearts. Our hearts control our motivation. God may convince our minds about many things, but until he enters our hearts and we understand what he wants, we'll remain unchanged.

So Jesus tells us to understand with our hearts and then uses the four types of soil to describe four conditions of the heart. The hard soil represents a hard heart. The rocky soil represents a superficial heart. The thorny soil represents a divided heart, and the good soil represents a willing heart. So far, so good. But here is where a new "ah ha" insight hit me.

Jesus, in teaching about four soils, was not talking about four types of people. I've taught for years that people have one of the four different heart types and we should change our hearts to contain the fourth soil. But, that's way too simplistic. No one totally fits in only one category of soil. The best-hearted among us is hard-hearted about some things, and the most stubborn person is willing-hearted about a few areas. What Jesus is saying is that each message or Kingdom teaching can be received in our hearts in one of four ways.

Pick any topic. Maybe it's giving. Maybe it's about loving your enemy (Matthew 5:44) or restoring a sinning brother or sister (Galatians 6:1) or holding to the commitments of marriage (Malachi 2:14; Hebrews 13:4). The topic, if it's presented accurately from Scripture, is not the point. The point is what will you do with it? Will you let it impact your heart?

Our hearts respond in one of four ways. Let's say, on the topic of giving, you hear a message on sacrifice or on giving a tenth of our income. Here's how your heart might process this.

If your heart is hard on the topic, then your heart, on this topic is hard soil. You decide to give the message minimal attention. You know that if you listen you might have to change. And that's not what you want to do.

If you don't dispute the accuracy of the teaching and you begin to follow it, but quit quickly, then on this topic, your heart is like rocky soil. It means your commitment to God is a mile wide and an inch deep. You think, "One of these days I'm going to start giving. I may even tithe. But not yet."

Or if you really buy in to the teaching about giving and decide, "Yes, I'm going to start tithing. That's what God wants. He'll bless me, too." But after making the decision you begin to have second thoughts then, on this topic, your heart is like thorny soil. You start to see how the 10 percent or more that you're giving is taking away from other things you would like to do. Plus, if you don't see an immediate increase in your income, you decide, "It didn't work." You allow divided loyalty to enter your heart and you back down from or even out of the commitment you once cherished.

But, finally if, when you hear the word, believe it, receive it, and obey it then, on this topic your heart is like good soil. God is on the move and you want to move with him.

See the distinction? It's not enough to understand with our minds, we must understand with our hearts. Once your heart is "on board" with God's ways, you're ready for the next step in preparing for a harvest.

Receiving the Teaching with Joy

Jesus begins his explanation: "When anyone hears the message about the Kingdom and does not understand it, the evil one comes and snatches away what was sown in his heart. This is the seed sown along the path" (Matthew 13:19). So the next action step, once you've heard with your mind and understood with your heart is to let your emotions catch up. Attitude is important in everything we think, feel, say, and do. I love the following story Dr. Charles Garfield tells about an encounter he had several years ago that illustrates the power of attitude.

Just Dance

If you have ever gone through a toll booth, you know that your relationship to the person in the booth is not the most intimate you'll ever have. It is one of life's frequent nonencounters: You hand over some money; you might get change; you drive off.

Late one morning in 1984, headed for lunch in San

Francisco, I drove toward a booth. I heard loud music. It sounded like a party. I looked around. No other cars with their windows open. No sound trucks. I looked at the toll booth. Inside it, the man was dancing.

"What are you doing?" I asked.

"I'm having a party," he said.

"What about the rest of the people?" I looked at the other toll booths.

"They look like . . . toll booths. What do they look like to you?"

He said, "Vertical coffins. At 8:30 every morning, live people get in. Then they die for eight hours. At 4:30, like Lazarus from the dead, they reemerge and go home. For eight hours, brain is on hold, dead on the job. Going through the motions."

I was amazed. This guy had developed a philosophy, a mythology about his job. Sixteen people dead on the job, and the seventeenth, in precisely the same situation, figures out a way to live. I could not help asking the next question: "Why is it different for you? You're having a good time."

He looked at me. "I knew you were going to ask that. I don't understand why anybody would think my job is boring. I have a corner office, glass on all sides. I can see the Golden Gate, San Francisco, and the Berkeley hills. Half the Western world vacations here

. . . and I just stroll in every day and practice dancing."[1]

I love that man's attitude. If he can be happy taking and making change, what does that say about us who are children of the God of the universe who owns everything and can make anything?

Celebrate God's Goodness

Our number one attitude as God's kids should be that he is a good God! The proof is all over the Bible. We've already seen over and over, how he's a good God in providing for us financially (Proverbs 3:9-10, Matthew 6:33, etc.). He is a good God in how he is so merciful to us: "But because of his great love for us, God, who is rich in mercy, made us alive with Christ even when we were dead in transgressions—it is by grace you have been saved" (Ephesians 2:4-5). He's a good God in giving us wisdom: "If any of you lacks wisdom, he should ask God, who gives generously to all without finding fault, and it will be given to him" (James 1:5). "But the wisdom that comes from heaven is first of all pure; then peace-loving, considerate, submissive, full of mercy and good fruit, impartial and sincere" (James 3:17). These brief examples illustrate and remind us that there is great power in celebrating the goodness of the Lord (Psalm 145:3-7):

Great is the LORD and most worthy of praise;
    his greatness no one can fathom.

One generation will commend your works to another;
    they will tell of your mighty acts.

They will speak of the glorious splendor of your

majesty, and I will meditate on your wonderful
works.

They will tell of the power of your awesome works,
and I will proclaim your great deeds.

They will celebrate your abundant goodness
and joyfully sing of your righteousness.

I'm sure you've heard the phrase, "Give until it hurts."
That's a terrible teaching. It totally misses God's heart. We
should receive teaching about increased giving with joy
because we're anticipating the wonderful things our great
and good God is going to do.

For example, one of the churches I've worked with had
a huge building campaign. They believed God wanted
them to relocate and in their relocation to also shift their
ministry emphasis toward outsiders. So they built an
excellent new building and only a few years later had seen
their attendance increase from about 300 to more than
800 each Sunday. In their new members' class they always
gave out a survey to help them see what drew the new
folks to the congregation. The vast majority responded
that the church building was the first thing that they
noticed and that they liked. Obviously, this congregation
has many other great ministries and relationship networks
going on or the people wouldn't stay, but their decision to
step out on the limb of faith and give to reach thousands
of new people for Jesus is one that God has rewarded.

Persevere through the Tough Times

Once we understand the Lord's teaching with our
hearts and joyfully begin to anticipate his working in

great new ways, we will have a new challenge to face. Jesus said, "But since he has no root, he lasts only a short time. When trouble or persecution comes because of the word, he quickly falls away" (Matthew 13:21). Once you make a commitment to give, get ready for challenges to come. In verse 19 Jesus mentioned that the devil tries to steal the teaching. When he fails at stealing this truth from your heart, he turns to attack you. The Bible says this opposition comes "because of the *word*." It's the same Greek word as "message" in verse 19. Receiving and following the message of the Kingdom on any topic does not mean we can enter into God's blessings without opposition. If anything, your obedience will cause Satan to send trouble or persecution. Why? To get you to stop! I like the old Texas phrase, "Dogs don't bark at parked cars." As long as you're "parked" and not moving forward with the Lord, the evil one has no reason to oppose you. He will turn his attention and the attention of his demons in other directions. He is not all-powerful like God, so he has to use his evil forces strategically (Ephesians 6:11-12). This is the reason why we often face more difficulties after we begin to follow through on any decision God wants us to make, including the area of giving. Do not despair if you feel under attack. It could mean that you're getting the attention of the devil but you're also going to see God come powerfully to your aid. Believe it.

Here's more detail on how the devil works. The first effort to get you to back off from following God in finances is through "troubles." This word literally means "difficulties" of all kinds. The devil may send problems that cause unexpected expenses or personal pain in your life circumstances simply because you're following God. Or, as Jesus continued, he may even use persecution to stall or turn back your efforts. Persecution is simply opposition to your decision. It could come from a friend or spouse who disagrees with your action of taking God at his word with your finances. The reality is that the devil will throw up road blocks to keep you from growing in this area. Why? Because he knows how dangerous it is to the kingdom of darkness when you give generously. He will do anything to stop you. He can't allow you to believe God will bless your efforts. He can't allow you to give so that others can be saved, encouraged, and blessed. He can't allow you to see for yourself, firsthand that God will release his power through you and bring a wonderful harvest.

So don't be surprised and don't be offended by the attacks. When I read the last phrase of verse 21 that evening, I felt a chill go through me. Jesus talked about the rocky soil heart being so superficial that he or she allows the difficulties to make them "fall away." I immediately grabbed my Greek New Testament to see what the original word was here. I found it is the same word used in other places in the Gospel of Matthew and translated "offended" (Matthew 15:12), to cause to sin (Matthew 18:6) or even to cease from following Jesus (Matthew 26:31). It's a powerful warning. Be prepared, but don't be afraid.

Gladys Aylward, missionary to China more than fifty years ago, was forced to flee when the Japanese invaded Yangcheng. But she could not leave her work behind. With only one assistant, she led more than a hundred orphans over the mountains toward Free China. In their book *The Hidden Price of Greatness,* Ray Besson and Ranelda Mack Hunsicker tell what happened:

> During Gladys's harrowing journey out of war-torn Yangcheng . . . she grappled with despair as never before. After passing a sleepless night, she faced the morning with no hope of reaching safety. A thirteen-year-old girl in the group reminded her of their much-loved story of Moses and the Israelites crossing the Red Sea. "But I am not Moses," Gladys cried in desperation. "Of course you aren't," the girl said, 'but Jehovah is still God!"[2]

When Gladys and the orphans made it through, they proved once again that no matter how inadequate we feel, God is still God, and we can trust in him.

Maintain God's Perspective on Money

The devil has a strategy for this whole journey of faith. First he tries to steal God's truth about giving from your heart. Failing that, he tries to steal your joy about giving. Failing that, he will attack you directly to make you stop. Failing that, he goes back to a clever, sneaky, stealth approach. He appeals to your normal, human desires for comfort, pleasure, and wealth. Don't fall for this trap either. Jesus said, "The one who received the seed that fell among the thorns is the man who hears the word, but the worries of this life and the deceitfulness of wealth choke it, making it unfruitful" (Matthew 13:22).

You and I must resist and reject man-made values about money. Jesus mentioned first the "worries of this life." It's very easy to see that Christians are not immune to experiencing stress about money, unpaid bills, or even concern about the future. One old country saying sums it up: "Worry is like a rocking chair. It gives you something to do but it won't get you anywhere." All it does is make you weak and sick.

Jesus also referred to the "deceitfulness of wealth." His use of the word wealth refers to the world's economic system. When you think about money, there are only four things you can do with it: make it, spend it, save it, or invest it. If you do any or all of these things using man-made values, you are wide open to deception, and the end result is not a pretty picture. Jesus said that these man-made perspectives cause two big problems. First, they will choke you spiritually. How many times have you seen someone who started tapering off his or her giving? At first the person feels uncomfortable with this decision. Later the discomfort turns into guilt and the guilt turns into apathy. Once apathy sets in concerning one area of our spiritual lives, it begins to seep over into others, as well. The result? No fruit.

The second problem is if you forget God's perspective on money you'll miss his harvest for you. And we've seen how extensive the blessings can be when God is in charge. Don't miss this blessing! Fight the devil's subtle schemes the same way you battle his head on assaults: Put God first.

Plan for a Crop

Once we take the first four action steps Jesus gave in Matthew 13, we have only one more left—and it's the fun one. Get ready for the harvest!

Jesus said, "But the one who received the seed that fell on good soil is the man who hears the word and understands it. He produces a crop, yielding a hundred, sixty or thirty times what was sown" (Matthew 13:23). Hear, understand, obey—you will see good things happen. God will take care of you and your needs. He will use your resources to bless and do good. And, best of all, he will fill you with a wonderful sense of his pleasure, presence, and power.

The only question is how big will the harvest be? Jesus said the crop will be thiry, sixty or even a hundred times what you sow. For you marketing and investment folks, that's a 3,000 percent, 6,000 percent, and 10,000 percent response rate. It demonstrates Jesus' promise that the harvest will be huge. Although God determines the exact dimensions of the harvest, you can definitely expect abundant blessing.

This final action step brings us right back to where we started four chapters ago. Give and it will be given to you. Let God prove his power to bless you. Take hold of true life. And expect a harvest. Do you believe God is able to do this? Are you convinced he is willing? Then take God at his word. Let your giving be your next step into a path of the Lord's power.

Notes:

[1] Dr. Charles Garfield, *Condensed Chicken Soup for the Soul* (Deerfield Beach, FL: Health Communications, Inc., 1991).
[2] Ray Besson and Ranelda Mack Hunsicker, *The Hidden Price of Greatness* (Carol Stream, IL: Tyndale House Publishers, 1991).

Think It Through
Expect a Harvest

1. This chapter tells us to "expect a harvest" when we give faithfully and prayerfully. What harvest from God are you expecting?

2. Of the four "heart conditions" presented in chapter four, which one might describe you in the area of giving?

   Hard heart

   Superficial heart

   Divided heart

   Willing heart

3. Read Matthew 13:23 again. "But the one who received the seed that fell on good soil is the man who hears the word and understands it. He produces a crop, yielding a hundred, sixty or thirty times what was sown." What three actions lead to producing a harvest?

   1.

   2.

   3.

4. How do you think the Lord wants you to put this chapter's teaching into practice?

About the Author

Dr. Kregg Hood, author, speaker, and educator, is executive vice president for Sweet Publishing. Dr. Hood has also served as a minister, a missionary, and a college instructor.

Hood earned his doctorate from Texas Tech University in instructional communication in 1987. He also holds master's degrees in missions and in religious communication and a bachelor of arts degree with undergraduate majors in Bible, biblical languages, and mathmatics.

He and his wife, Karen, are parents of a daughter, Kalah, and a son, Kyle.

Dr. Hood is available to teach or speak for special events and may be contacted by phone, 1-800-531-5220, or by fax, 1-817-232-2030.